MW00595435

THE WIND BENEATH MY WINGS

& 25 Contemporary Movie Themes

Easy Piano Arrangements by DAN COATES

CONTENTS

THE WIND BENEATH MY WINGS

Words and Music by
LARRY HENLEY and JEFF SILBAR
Arranged by DAN COATES

3

5

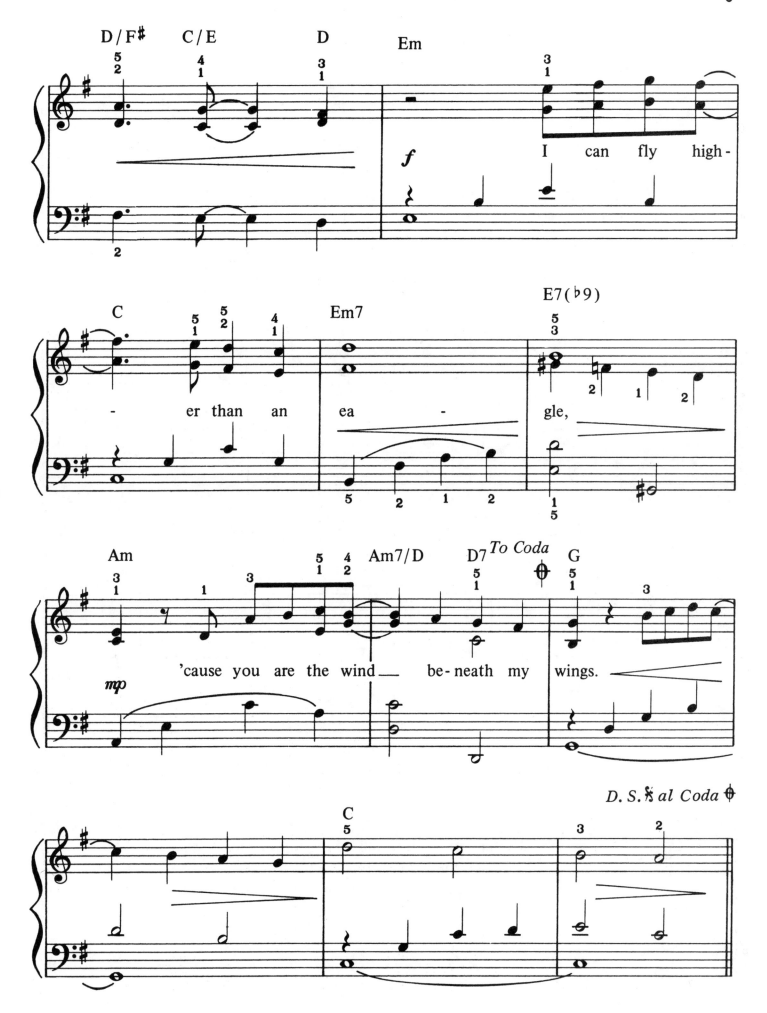

6

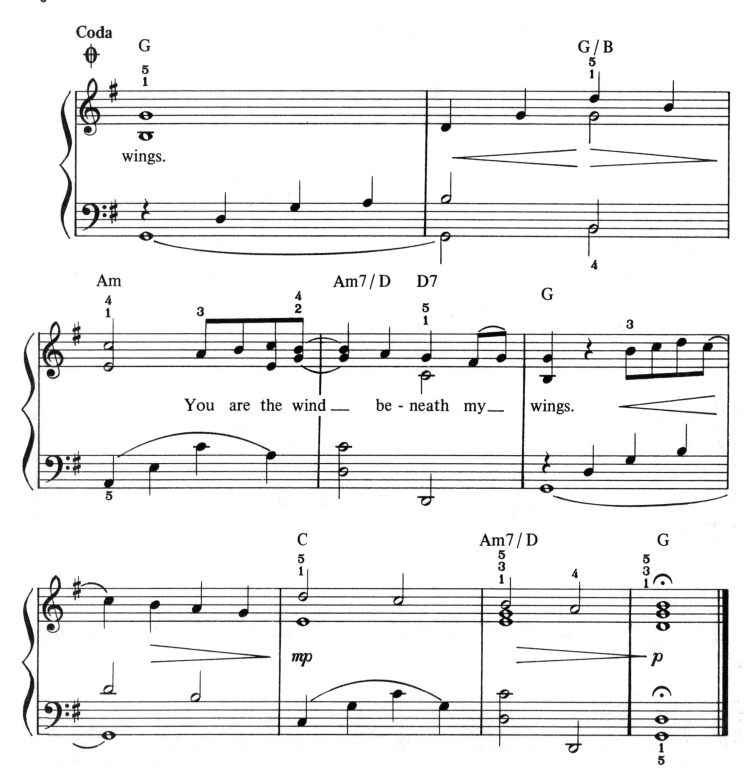

3. It might have appeared to go unnoticed
   But I've got it all here in my heart.
   I want you to know I know the truth:
   I would be nothing without you.

LET THE RIVER RUN

(Theme from "Working Girl")

Words and Music by
CARLY SIMON
Arranged by DAN COATES

8

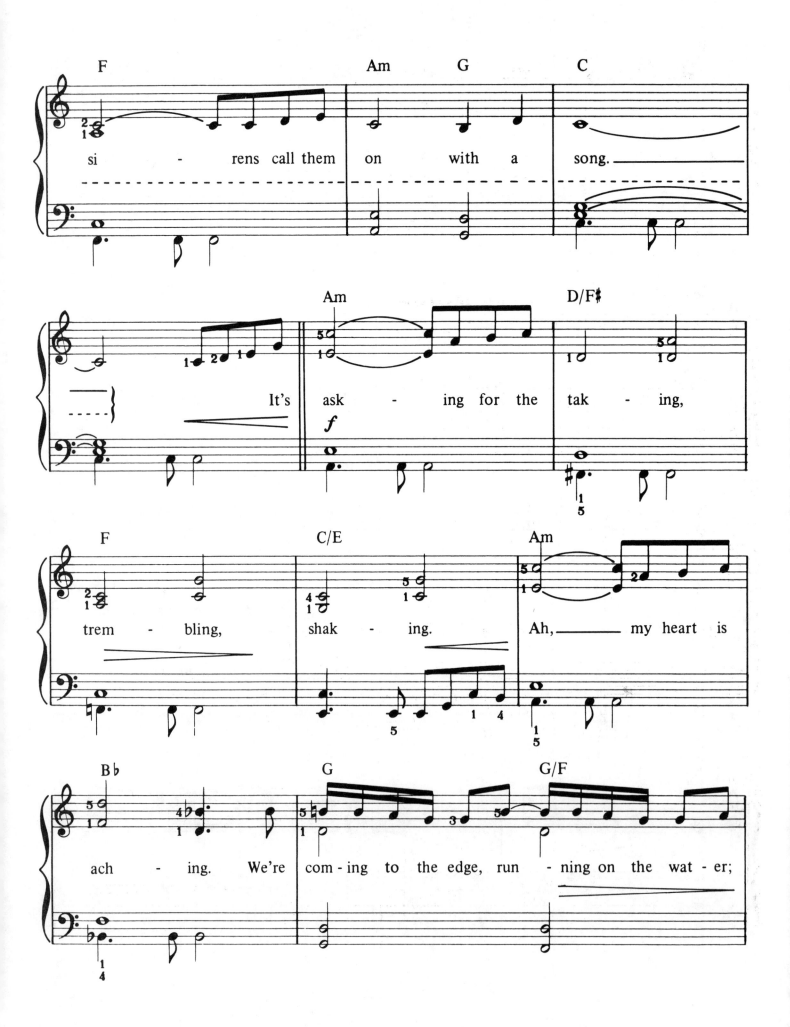

9

Coda

Let _____ the riv - er run, _____ let all the

dream - ers wake the na - tion.

Come, the new Je - ru - sa - lem.

THE BATMAN THEME
From the Motion Picture BATMAN™

Music Composed by
DANNY ELFMAN
Arranged by DAN COATES

Moderately Slow

14

16

I WILL ALWAYS LOVE YOU
(From the Motion Picture "THE BODYGUARD")

Words and Music by
DOLLY PARTON
Arranged by DAN COATES

18

Extra Lyrics:

3. I hope life treats you kind
And I hope you have all you've dreamed of.
I wish you joy and happiness.
But above all this,
I wish you love.

PACHELBEL CANON IN D

By
JOHANN PACHELBEL
Arranged by DAN COATES

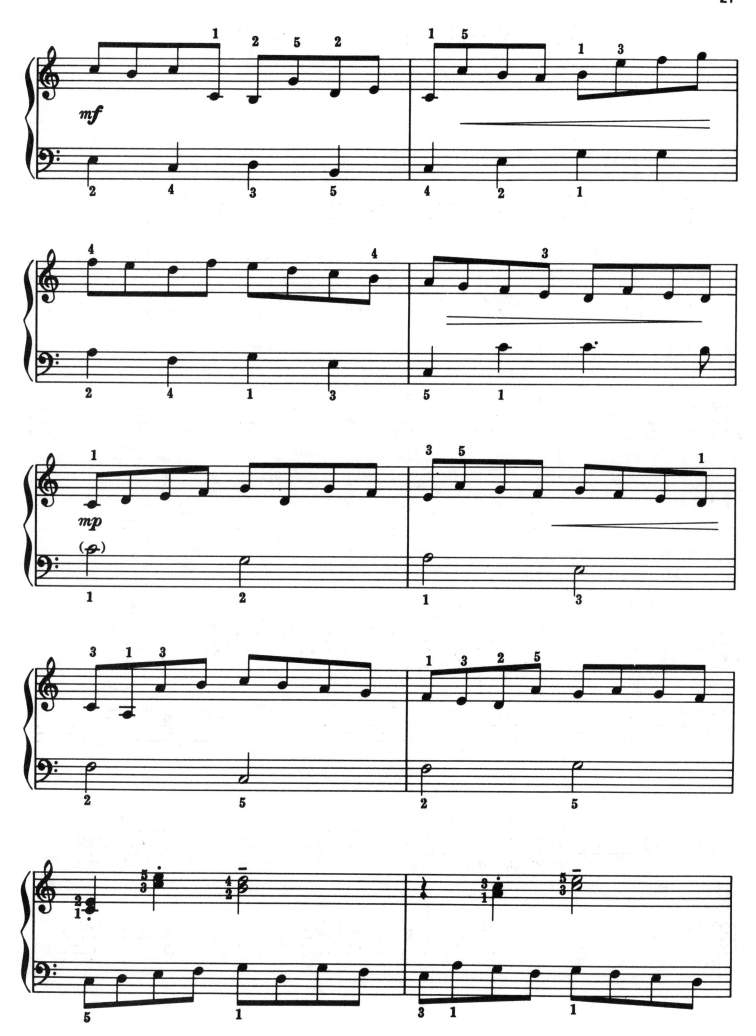

25

SONG FROM M*A*S*H
(Suicide Is Painless)

Words and Music by
MIKE ALTMAN and JOHNNY MANDEL
Arranged by DAN COATES

Through ear - ly morn - ing fog I see

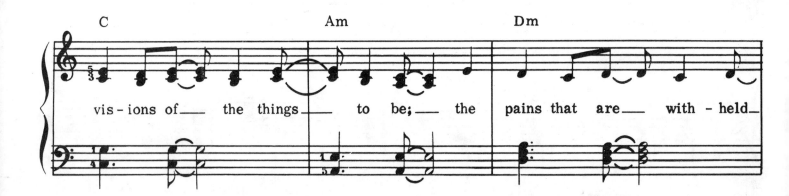

vis - ions of the things to be; the pains that are with - held

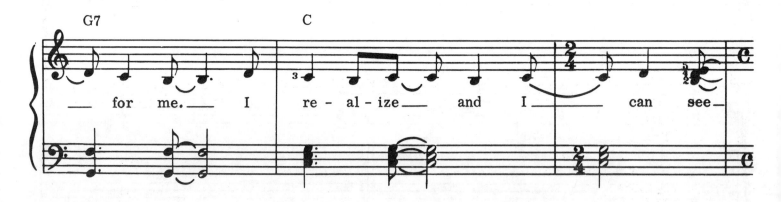

for me. I re - al - ize and I can see

that su - i - cide is pain -

1. Try to find a way to make
   All our little joys relate
   Without that ever-present hate
   But now I know that it's too late.
   And -(Chorus)

3. The game of life is hard to play,
   I'm going to lose it anyway,
   The losing card I'll someday lay,
   So this is all I have to say,
   That -(Chorus)

4. The only way to win, is cheat
   And lay it down before I'm beat,
   And to another give a seat
   For that's the only painless feat.
   'Cause: -(Chorus)

5. The sword of time will pierce our skins,
   It doesn't hurt when it begins
   But as it works its way on in,
   The pain grows stronger, watch it grin.
   For: -(Chorus)

6. A brave man once requested me
   To answer questions that are key,
   Is it to be or not to be
   And I replied; "Oh, why ask me."
   'Cause: -(Chorus)

LA BAMBA

Adaptation by
RITCHIE VALENS
Arranged by DAN COATES

"Latin Rock" beat

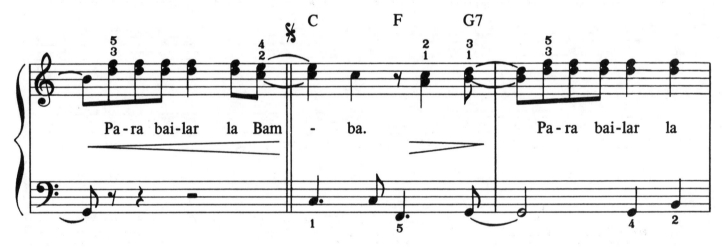

Pa - ra bai-lar la Bam - ba.   Pa - ra bai-lar la

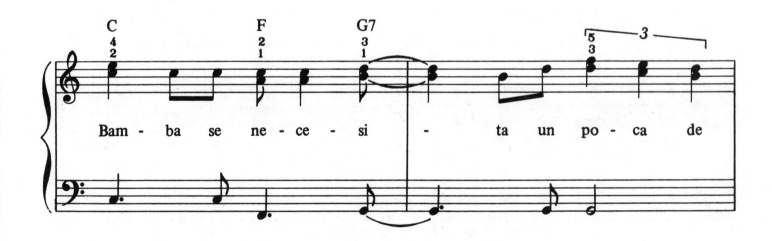

Bam - ba se ne - ce - si - ta un po - ca de

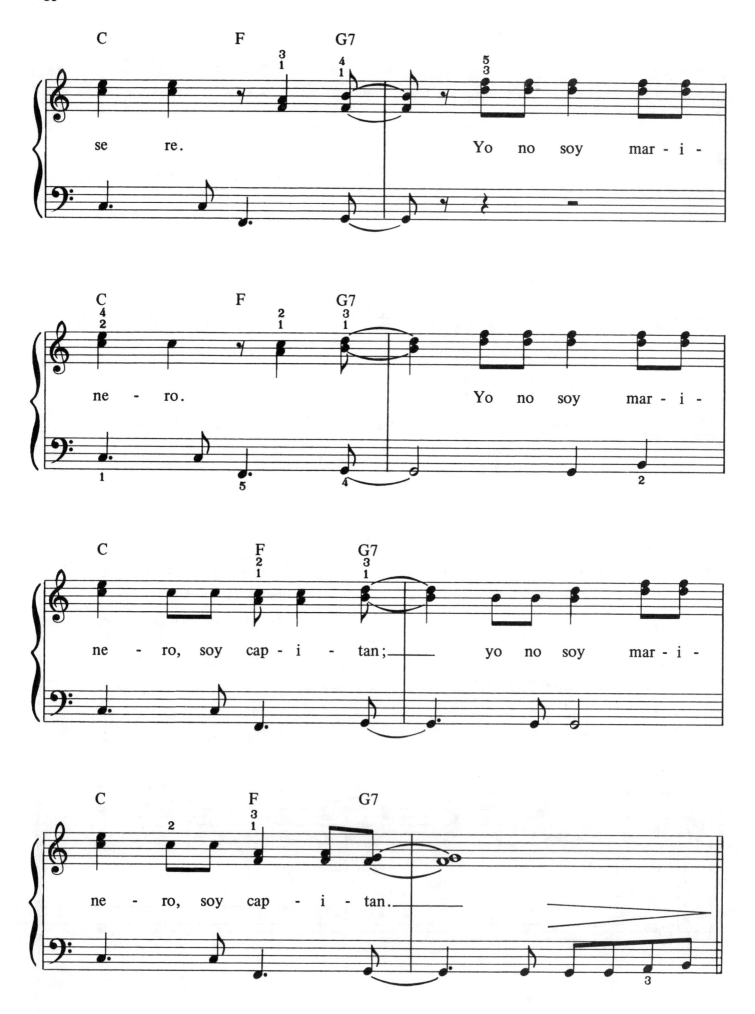

CAN YOU READ MY MIND
Love Theme from "SUPERMAN" A Warner Bros. film

Words by
LESLIE BRICUSSE

Music by
JOHN WILLIAMS
Arranged by DAN COATES

33

LEAN ON ME

Words and Music by
BILL WITHERS
Arranged by DAN COATES

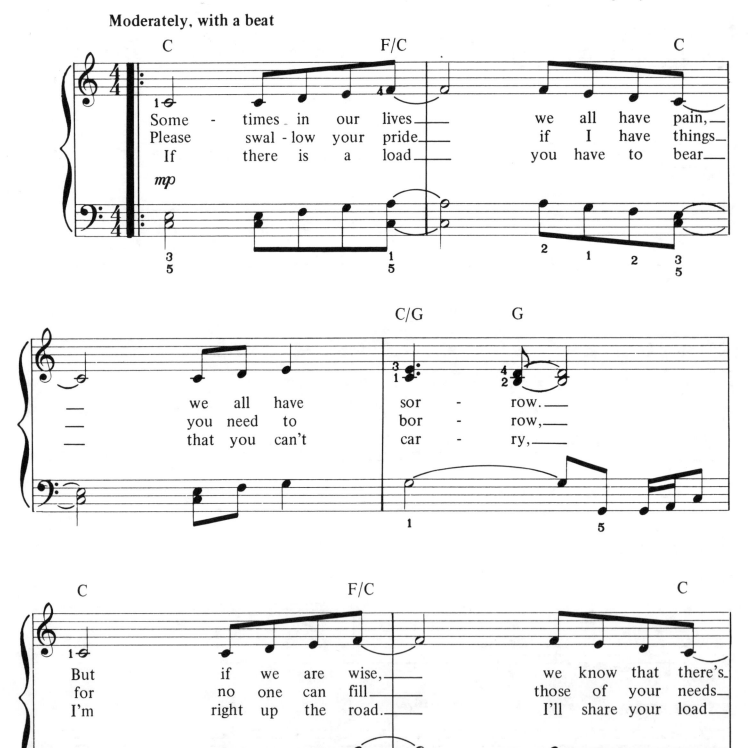

TWO HEARTS
(From The Motion Picture Soundtrack "BUSTER")

Words by
PHIL COLLINS

Music by
LAMONT DOZIER
Arranged by DAN COATES

rea - son to be-lieve___ she'll al - ways be there.

42

44

far a-part__ we are,__ she knows,__

D.S. 𝄋 *al Coda* ⊕

I'm al-ways right there be-side.__ her.

cresc.

Coda

Extra Lyrics:

Well there's no easy way to, to understand it
There's so much of my life in her
And it's like I planned it
And it teaches you to never let go
There's so much love you'll never know
She can reach you no matter how far
Wherever you are.

(Chorus:)

THAT'S WHAT FRIENDS ARE FOR

Words and Music by
BURT BACHARACH and CAROLE BAYER SAGER
Arranged by DAN COATES

49

LIVE TO TELL

Words and Music by
MADONNA CICCONE and PAT LEONARD
Arranged by DAN COATES

Moderate Rock ballad

52

THIS USED TO BE MY PLAYGROUND

Words and Music by
MADONNA CICCONE and SHEP PETTIBONE
Arranged by DAN COATES

Slowly, with expression

58

MISS CELIE'S BLUES (Sister)

Words by
QUINCY JONES, ROD TEMPERTON
and LIONEL RICHIE

Music by
QUINCY JONES and ROD TEMPERTON
Arranged by DAN COATES

Slow and bluesy

Sis - ter,____ you've been on my mind,____ sis - ter,____ we're

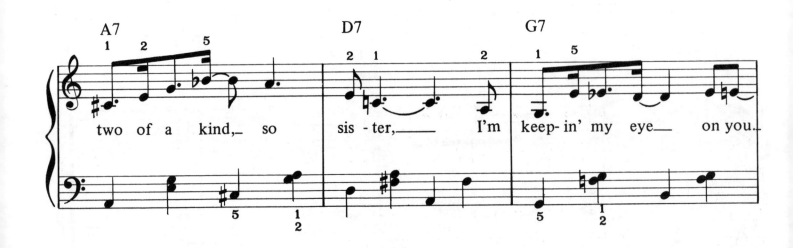

two of a kind,__ so sis - ter,____ I'm keep- in' my eye__ on you.

62

SEND IN THE CLOWNS
From "A LITTLE NIGHT MUSIC"

Words and Music by
STEPHEN SONDHEIM
Arranged by DAN COATES

Slowly, with expression

66

Theme from
"LOVE AFFAIR"

Music by
ENNIO MORRICONE
Arranged by DAN COATES

Gentle, flowing

SEPARATE LIVES
(Love Theme From "WHITE NIGHTS")

Words and Music by
STEPHEN BISHOP
Arranged by DAN COATES

Freely, with expression

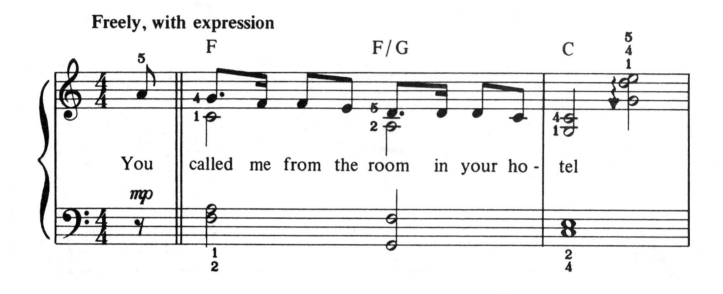

You called me from the room in your ho-tel

all full of ro-mance for some-one you had met, and

tell-ing me how sor-ry you were leav-ing so soon, and that you

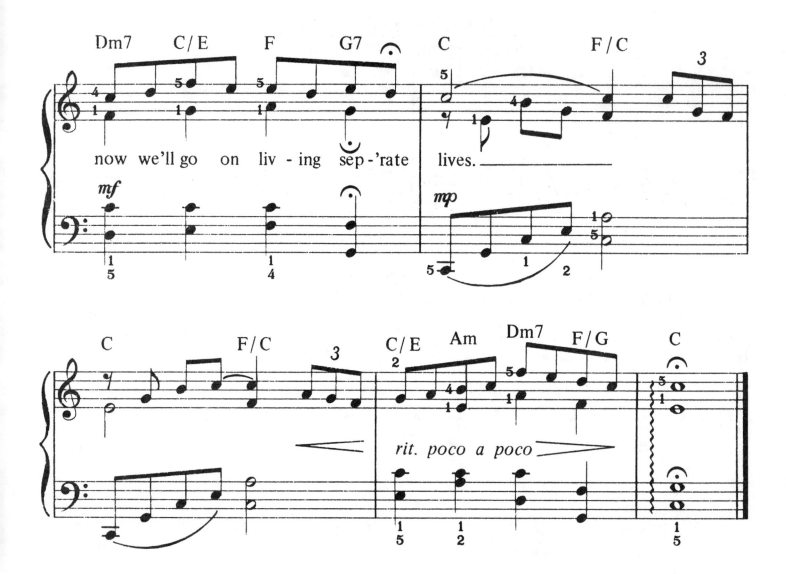

now we'll go on liv - ing sep -'rate lives.

Chorus 2:

Well, I held on to let you go.
And if you lost your love for me,
You never let it show.
There was no way to compromise.
So now we're living separate lives.

Chorus 3:

You have no right to ask me how I feel.
You have no right to speak to me so kind.
Someday I might find myself looking in your eyes.
But for now, we'll go on living separate lives.
Yes, for now we'll go on living separate lives.

GLORY OF LOVE
(Theme from THE KARATE KID Part II)

Words and Music by
DAVID FOSTER, PETER CETERA and DIANE NINI
Arranged by DAN COATES

To-night it's ver-y clear, as we're both stand-ing here, there's so man-y things I want to say I will al-ways love you,— I will nev-er leave you a-

HOW DO YOU KEEP THE MUSIC PLAYING?

(From the Warner Bros. Motion Picture "BEST FRIENDS")

Words by
ALAN and MARILYN BERGMAN

Music by
MICHEL LEGRAND
Arranged by DAN COATES

Moderate Ballad

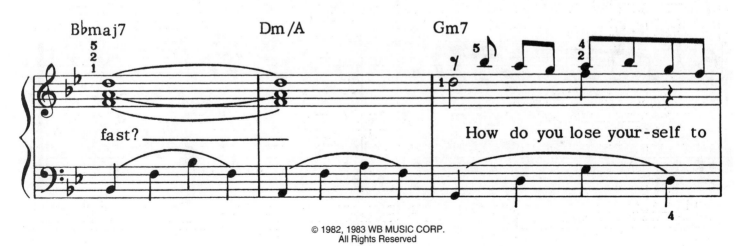

83

THEME FROM "SUPERMAN"
A WARNER BROS. film

By
JOHN WILLIAMS
Arranged by DAN COATES

Majestically

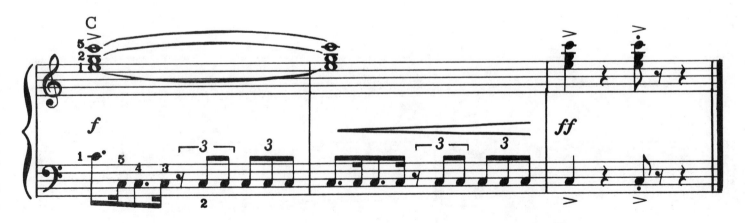

THE ROSE

Words and Music by
AMANDA McBROOM
Arranged by DAN COATES

flow - er _____ and you _____ it's on - ly seed.

poco cresc.

It's the heart _____ a - fraid of
night _____ has been too

mf

break - ing _____ that nev-er_ learns to dance. It's the
lone - ly and the road_ has been too long, and you

dream _____ a - fraid of wak - ing _____ that nev-er_ takes the
think _____ that love is on - ly for the luck-y_ and the

89

STAND BY ME

Words and Music by
JERRY LEIBER, MIKE STOLLER
and BEN E. KING
Arranged by DAN COATES

Moderately Slow

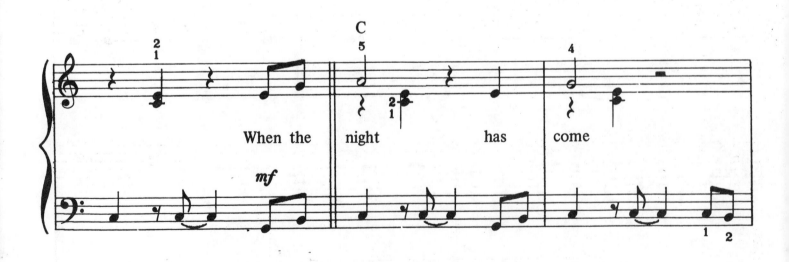

When the night has come

LANE'S THEME
(From the Original Motion Picture Soundtrack ''8 SECONDS'')

Composed by
BILL CONTI
Arranged by DAN COATES

THE THORN BIRDS THEME

By
HENRY MANCINI
Arranged by DAN COATES

STAR WARS
(Main Theme)
From the LUCASFILM LTD Production/TWENTIETH CENTURY-FOX Releases "STAR WARS",
"THE EMPIRE STRIKES BACK" & "RETURN OF THE JEDI"

Music by
JOHN WILLIAMS
Arranged by DAN COATES

THEME FROM A SUMMER PLACE

Words by
MACK DISCANT

Music by
MAX STEINER